ope you enjoy this boo...

...urn or re...

Harry Potter™

HERMIONE GRANGER™

CINEMATIC GUIDE

SCHOLASTIC LTD.

www.harrypotter.com

Scholastic Children's Books
Euston House, 24 Eversholt Street,
London NW1 1DB, UK

A division of Scholastic Ltd
London ~ New York ~ Toronto ~ Sydney ~ Auckland
Mexico City ~ New Delhi ~ Hong Kong

First published in the US by Scholastic Inc, 2016
Published in the UK by Scholastic Ltd, 2016

By Felicity Baker
Art Direction: Rick DeMonico
Page Design: Two Red Shoes Design

ISBN 978 1407 17316 0

Printed and bound in Germany

2 4 6 8 10 9 7 5 3 1

Papers used by Scholastic Children's Books are made from
wood grown in sustainable forests.

www.scholastic.co.uk

Contents

Film Beginnings

Hermione Granger grew up in a Muggle family who were proud when she got her letter from Hogwarts. From the moment she boarded the Hogwarts Express as a first year, she showed a talent for magic and spellwork.

In the first Harry Potter film, Hermione meets Harry and Ron on the Hogwarts Express, a train that brings students from King's Cross station in London to Hogwarts castle at the start of each school year.

"*You're Harry Potter, aren't you?
I know all about you, of course.*"

– HERMIONE GRANGER, *HARRY POTTER
AND THE PHILOSOPHER'S STONE* FILM

Hermione makes quite an impression when she enters Ron and Harry's train compartment.

Hermione casts a spell to fix Harry's broken glasses with the words "Oculus Reparo."

Hermione and all the other first-year students disembark from the train and take boats across the lake to get to Hogwarts castle.

Hogwarts School of Witchcraft and Wizardry becomes a second home to Hermione. Over her six years at Hogwarts, she earns a reputation both for her dazzling intelligence and eagerness to help others.

Life at Hogwarts

After their arrival at Hogwarts, it's time to get sorted. Each student is placed into one of the four houses: Gryffindor, Hufflepuff, Ravenclaw or Slytherin.

Hermione is clever enough to be sorted into Ravenclaw, but, as she hoped, she's placed in Gryffindor.

Harry and Ron are also sorted into Gryffindor.

When they first meet, it doesn't seem as though Hermione, Harry and Ron will get along.

"Stop, stop, stop! You're going to take someone's eye out. Besides, you're saying it wrong. It's Leviosa not Leviosa."

– HERMIONE GRANGER, HARRY POTTER AND THE PHILOSOPHER'S STONE FILM

A dangerous event forges the start of Hermione,
Harry and Ron's extraordinary friendship.

Hermione is in the bathroom when a giant troll wanders in!
Harry and Ron hear a troll is on the loose and go looking for
Hermione to warn her.

Harry and Ron defeat the troll just in time. When the teachers appear and see that Harry and Ron have broken the rules by fighting the troll, Hermione takes the blame.

Hermione quickly proves herself
to be a clever and dedicated student by
excelling in all of her subjects.

"*Do you take pride in being an insufferable know-it-all? Five points from Gryffindor!*"

– PROFESSOR SNAPE TO HERMIONE,
*HARRY POTTER AND THE
PRISONER OF AZKABAN* FILM

Hermione's teachers take notice of her intelligence and love of learning.

"Well, well, well, Hermione, you really are the brightest witch of your age I've ever met."

– PROFESSOR LUPIN,
*HARRY POTTER AND THE
PRISONER OF AZKABAN* FILM

"They've yet to think of a spell that our Hermione can't do."

– RUBEUS HAGRID,
*HARRY POTTER AND
THE CHAMBER OF
SECRETS* FILM

But not all classes are easy for Hermione. In her third year, Hermione discovers the one Hogwarts subject she doesn't care for: Divination, the art of divining the future. Hermione prefers logical subjects without so much guesswork.

"From the first moment you stepped foot in my class, I sensed that you did not possess the proper spirit for the noble art of Divination."

– Professor Trelawney, *Harry Potter and the Prisoner of Azkaban* film

Hermione occasionally takes a break from her studies to have fun. She becomes the talk of Hogwarts when she attends the Yule Ball with famous Quidditch player Viktor Krum from Durmstrang.

Ron is jealous that Hermione goes to the Yule Ball with Viktor instead of with him.

"*Next time there's a ball, pluck up the courage to ask me before somebody else does and not as a last resort!*"

– HERMIONE GRANGER, *HARRY POTTER AND THE GOBLET OF FIRE* FILM

Hermione starts off her time at Hogwarts as a stickler for the rules. However, as she gets older, she finds the value in breaking them occasionally.

"Now if you two don't mind, I'm going to bed before either of you come up with another clever idea to get us killed – or worse, expelled."

– HERMIONE GRANGER, *HARRY POTTER AND THE PHILOSOPHER'S STONE* FILM

> *"It's sort of exciting, isn't it? Breaking the rules."*
>
> – HERMIONE GRANGER, *HARRY POTTER AND THE ORDER OF THE PHOENIX* FILM

Family, Friends and Foes

Hermione makes many friends in the wizarding world, including Harry, Ron and other fellow students. Hermione is a fierce and loyal friend who will stop at nothing to protect the people she cares about – even if that means putting herself in danger.

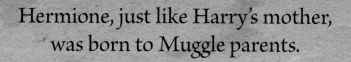

Hermione, just like Harry's mother,
was born to Muggle parents.

Hermione comes from an ordinary and loving family.

Hermione: "My parents are dentists.
They tend to people's teeth."

Professor Slughorn: "Fascinating,
and is that considered a dangerous
profession?"

– HARRY POTTER AND THE HALF-BLOOD PRINCE FILM

Hermione is often teased about having non-magical parents, especially by Draco Malfoy, who calls her a "Mudblood."

"There are some wizards – like the Malfoy family – who think they're better than everyone else because they're what people call pureblood."

– Rubeus Hagrid, *Harry Potter and the Chamber of Secrets* film

Draco and his friends.

Hermione's parents are proud she's a witch. However, she wipes their memories to keep them out of danger from Lord Voldemort's Death Eaters.

"Obliviate."

– HERMIONE GRANGER,
HARRY POTTER AND THE
DEATHLY HALLOWS –
PART 1 FILM

Hermione comforts her friends when they are upset.

In Defence Against the Dark Arts class, Mad-Eye Moody demonstrates the Cruciatus Curse, a torture spell that was used on Neville Longbottom's parents. After class, Hermione comforts Neville.

Hermione gives Harry a pep talk before he competes in the Triwizard Tournament.

Hermione: "The key is to concentrate. After that you just have to–"

Harry: "Battle a dragon."

– HARRY POTTER AND THE GOBLET OF FIRE FILM

Hermione sticks by her friends' sides, even when there's danger.

In their sixth year, Hermione stays by Ron's hospital bedside after he accidentally drinks poison meant for Professor Dumbledore and ends up in the hospital wing.

When Hermione thinks that Sirius Black, an escapee from
Azkaban prison, wants to hurt Harry, she puts herself in harm's
way to protect him from danger.

*"If you want to kill Harry, you'll have
to kill us, too."*

– HERMIONE GRANGER, *HARRY POTTER*
AND THE PRISONER OF AZKABAN FILM

Hermione refuses to let Harry search for Lord Voldemort's hidden Horcruxes on his own. Hermione knows she needs to be by her friend's side on such a dangerous mission.

"You don't really think you're going to be able to find all those Horcruxes by yourself, do you? You need us."

– HERMIONE GRANGER, *HARRY POTTER AND THE HALF-BLOOD PRINCE* FILM

Hermione refuses to divulge any secrets about their Horcrux hunt – even under torture by Bellatrix Lestrange, a vicious Death Eater.

Hermione is protective of the people she cares about most. She stands up for Hagrid and Buckbeak when Draco makes light of the Hippogriff's impending execution.

"You foul, loathsome, evil little cockroach!"

– HERMIONE GRANGER, *HARRY POTTER AND THE PRISONER OF AZKABAN* FILM

Cleverest Moments

Hermione is known at Hogwarts as the brightest witch of her age. On her many adventures with Harry and Ron, it is often thanks to Hermione's educated mind, grasp of logic and quick thinking that the trio safely escapes and succeeds.

Hermione often saves the day by applying what she has learned in class to sticky situations.

Hermione is the one who realizes that Hagrid's three-headed dog, Fluffy, is standing on top of the trapdoor guarding the Philosopher's Stone.

Hermione uses her knowledge of Herbology, especially dangerous plants, to help Harry find the Philosopher's Stone hidden in Hogwarts castle.

"Devil's Snare, Devil's Snare ... 'It's deadly fun ... but will sulk in the sun!' That's it!"

– HERMIONE GRANGER, *HARRY POTTER AND THE PHILOSOPHER'S STONE* FILM

In their second year, Professor Lockhart frees a cage full of Cornish pixies in Defence Against the Dark Arts class.

Hermione is the only one who knows the spell that can stop the mischievous little creatures.

"Immobulus!"

– HERMIONE GRANGER, *HARRY POTTER AND THE CHAMBER OF SECRETS* FILM

Over the years, Hermione becomes an expert at brewing Polyjuice Potion, which allows the user to take on another person's appearance.

Hermione uses Polyjuice Potion to impersonate Death Eater Bellatrix Lestrange.

She also uses it to sneak into the Ministry of Magic with Harry and Ron.

Through research at the library, Hermione discovers that the mysterious beast in the Chamber of Secrets is a Basilisk, also known as the King of Serpents.

Anyone who looks a Basilisk *directly* in the eye will perish.

Hermione sees the Basilisk *indirectly* in a mirror. She survives, but is Petrified – literally turned to stone.

Before being Petrified, Hermione left a clue about the Basilisk
for Harry and Ron to find.

Thanks to Hermione, Harry is able to defeat the Basilisk and
save Hogwarts from its terror and destruction.

Hermione uses a Time-Turner to go back
in time to save Hagrid's Hippogriff, Buckbeak,
and Harry's godfather, Sirius Black.

Hermione and Harry watch as past events unfold.

While on the run with Harry and Ron, Hermione puts an Undetectable Extension Charm on her small, purple bag. That way Hermione can be prepared for any situation.

The charm allows the inside of the bag to expand to fit whatever she needs to carry, while appearing to be its original size on the outside.

She keeps a magical tent in the bag that comes in very handy while they are hunting for Horcruxes.

When Ron gets Splinched after Disapparating from the Ministry, Hermione uses the Essence of Dittany she keeps in her bag to heal his wounds.

When Harry, Ron and Hermione break into Gringotts in disguise to find a Horcrux, their cover is blown and Hermione must find a way to get them out alive.

Hermione: "Who's got an idea?"

Ron: "You're the brilliant one."

Hermione: "I've got something, but it's mad!"

– HARRY POTTER AND THE
DEATHLY HALLOWS – PART 2 FILM

Hermione daringly jumps onto the fire-breathing dragon that guards the Gringotts vaults. It bursts through the roof, soaring through the sky with Hermione, Ron and Harry holding on for their lives.

Fighting Dark Forces

Hermione's determination and pluck, combined with her brilliance at spells, make her one of Harry Potter's strongest allies. She fights by his side at a number of important battles.

In her fifth year, Hermione has the idea to start the secret group Dumbledore's Army to teach her fellow students how to defend themselves against Dark magic.

Hermione convinces Harry to teach their classmates defensive magic.

"We've got to be able to defend ourselves. And if Umbridge refuses to teach us how, we need someone who will."

– HERMIONE GRANGER, *HARRY POTTER AND THE ORDER OF THE PHOENIX* FILM

During a DA session, students learn to produce a Patronus, a spell that wards off Dementors.

Members of Dumbledore's Army have their skills put to the test.

When a group of Snatchers discovers Hermione, Harry and Ron's hiding place in the woods, Hermione thinks fast and figures out a way to buy them time to disguise who they truly are.

Hermione uses a spell to make Harry's face swell, making it difficult for the Snatchers to recognize him.

The Snatchers take them to Malfoy Manor in the hope that
Draco will be able to identify his former classmates.

Hermione plays a crucial part in the final
battle of Hogwarts and Lord Voldemort's
ultimate downfall.

Hermione and Ron go into the Chamber of Secrets in
search of a Basilisk fang that will destroy the lost diadem of
Ravenclaw, a Horcrux.

Hermione and Ron are so relieved to be alive they finally admit their true feelings for each other and kiss.

"We wouldn't last two days
without her."

– Ron Weasley, *Harry Potter and
the Deathly Hallows – Part 2* film